PIANO / VOCAL / GUITAR

KILLING ME SOFTLY WITH HIS SONG
HAPPY DAYS & THE GREAT SONGS OF
CHARLES FOX

Cover photo by Annamaria DiSanto

ISBN 0-634-09293-6

HAL•LEONARD®
CORPORATION

7777 W. BLUEMOUND RD. P.O. BOX 13819 MILWAUKEE, WI 53213

Visit Hal Leonard Online at
www.halleonard.com

CHARLES FOX

Charles Fox was born and raised in New York City, graduated from the High School of Music and Art, and continued his formal musical education with Nadia Boulanger in Paris. He studied jazz piano with Lenny Tristano and electronic music with Vladimir Ussachevsky at Columbia University.

He has composed the musical scores for over 100 motion pictures and television films, including *Barbarella, Nine to Five, Goodbye Columbus* and *Foul Play*, for which he received one of his two Academy Award nominations. The other nomination was for the film *The Other Side of the Mountain*. Among his popular songs are "Ready to Take a Chance Again," "I Got a Name" and "Killing Me Softly with His Song," for which he received the Grammy® Award for Best Song. TV shows for which he wrote theme songs include "The Love Boat," "Happy Days," "Laverne and Shirley," "Wonder Woman," "The Paper Chase," and "Love American Style," for which he received *two* Emmy Awards, for the score as well as the theme song.

Among the many legendary and diverse recording artists who have recorded his songs are Roberta Flack, Sarah Vaughan, Barry Manilow, Jim Croce, Fred Astaire, Luther Vandross, Johnny Cash, Lena Horne, George Shearing, the Boston Pops, Jack Jones, Dionne Warwick, Tito Puente, Goldie Hawn, Carly Simon, Johnny Mathis, Shirley Bassey, Crystal Gayle, Lori Lieberman, Sergio Mendes, Maureen McGovern, Olivia Newton-John, Lauryn Hill & The Fugees, and Ice T.

Charles has had a long-term collaboration with lyricist Norman Gimbel and as well with Hal David. He has also collaborated with Paul Williams, Bob Crewe, David Zippel, Sammy Cahn, Carly Simon, and Carol Bayer Sager.

In addition to his popular work, Charles has composed music for the concert hall and ballet. His ballet *A Song for Dead Warriors* was originally composed for the San Francisco Ballet and continues to be performed by the Dance Theatre of Harlem. His ballet *Zorro!* was premiered in San Francisco with the Smuin Ballet in 2003. He has also written numerous other works for orchestra, chorus, and chamber groups, including the orchestral suite, *Victory at Entebbe*.

Charles was awarded the 1992 BMI Richard Kirk Award for outstanding life achievement in music. He was inducted into the Songwriters Hall of Fame in 2004.

Charles Fox, Fred Astaire

Hal David, Paul Williams, Charles Fox

Andy Williams, Charles Fox

Songwriters Hall of Fame induction ceremony

with his wife, Joan

conducting the Kanagawa Philharmonic, Tokyo

cast of Charles Fox Songbook concert

AND THE FEELING'S GOOD

Words by NORMAN GIMBEL
Music by CHARLES FOX

* Guitarists, play chords finger style

On my way___

ing's good,___ know-ing now I've got a love to give___ out. Yes, the feel-

ing's good,___ it's a groov-y kind of life to live___ out. Oh, it feels___

___ so good___ to know the joys___ the songs___ keep sing - ing of.___ And the feel-

AS LONG AS IT'S YOU

Words by HAL DAVID
Music by CHARLES FOX

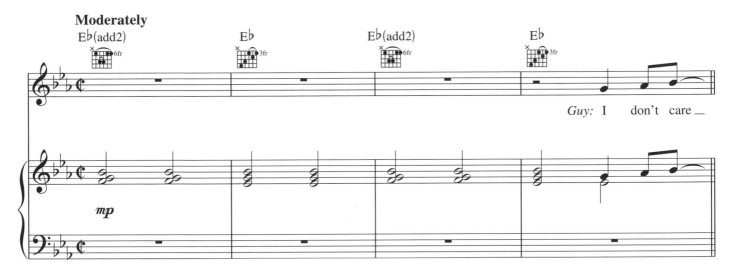

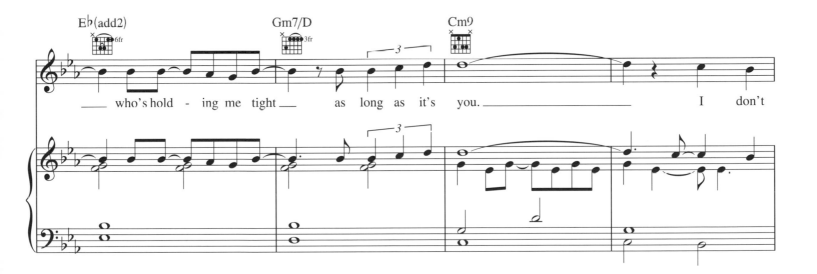

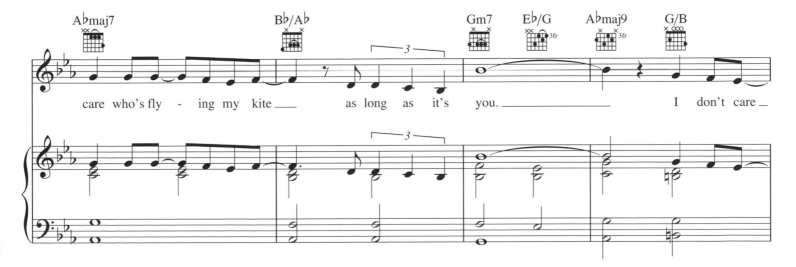

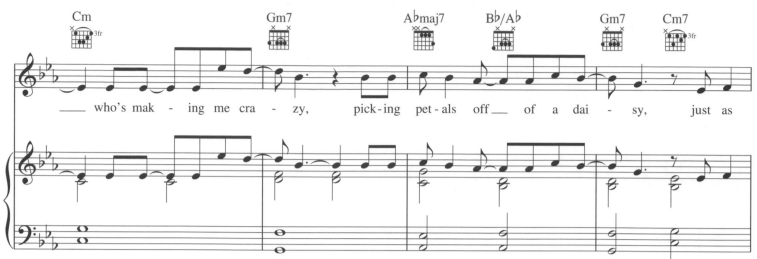

_____ who's mak - ing me cra - zy, pick-ing pet - als off _____ of a dai - sy, just as

long as when _ she's done _____ it turns out _____ that I'm _____ the one _

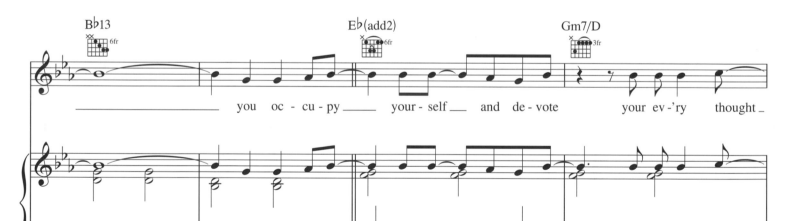

_____ you oc - cu - py _____ your - self _____ and de - vote _____ your ev - 'ry thought _

_____ to. _____ I don't care who's row - ing my boat _____ as long as it's

THEME FROM "BARBARELLA"
from the Motion Picture BARBARELLA

Words by BOB CREWE
Music by CHARLES FOX

ev - er　　we're　to - geth - er　the

Plan - ets　all　stand　still.

Refrain

Bar - ba - rel - la,　psy - che - del - la,　there's a kind of cock-

- le shell　a - bout　you.

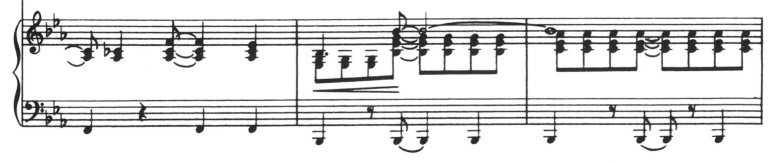

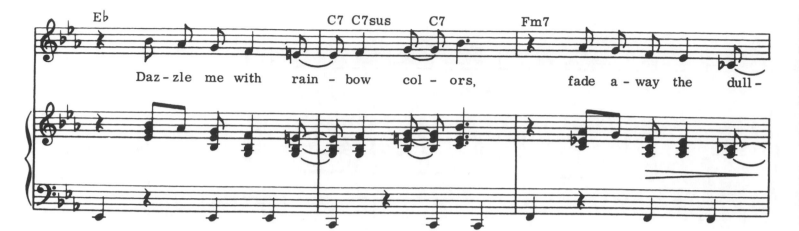

Daz-zle me with rain-bow col-ors, fade a-way the dull-

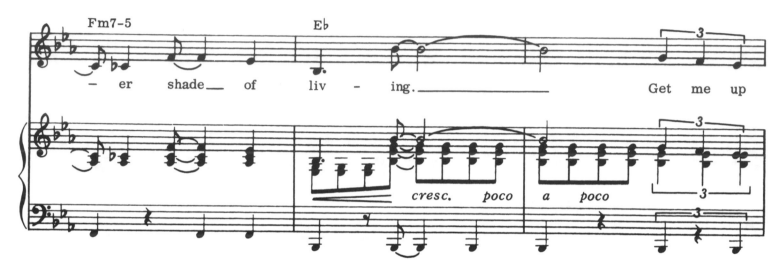

— er shade__ of liv - ing._____ Get me up

high,_____ teach me to fly,_____

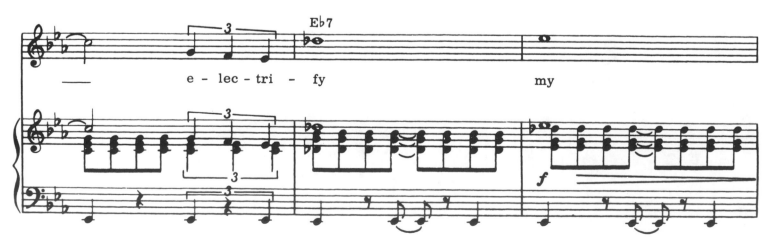

— e - lec - tri - fy my

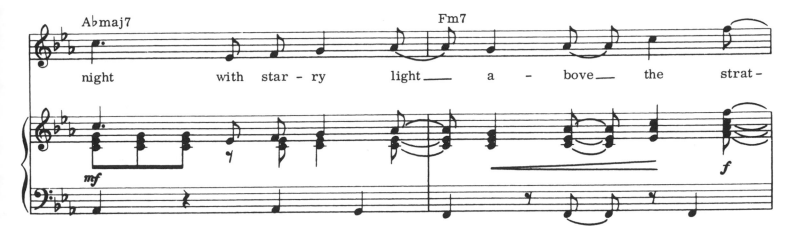

night with star - ry light___ a - bove__ the strat -

__ o - sphere._____ Bring your dear - ness near__

__ 'til the dawn comes tum - bling down. (Don't_ make a

dim. *poco* *a* *poco*

sound.) Ev - 'ry word_ we need_ comes from__ the skies.__

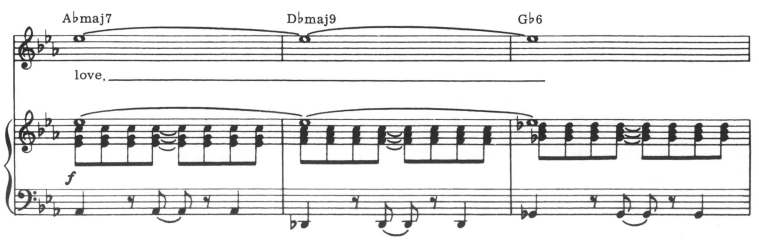

Keep repeating and fade out

GIRL
from the Paramount Film STAR SPANGLED GIRL

Words by NORMAN GIMBEL
Music by CHARLES FOX

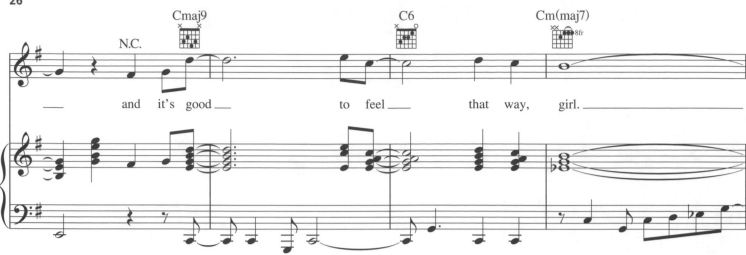

and it's good ___ to feel ___ that way, girl. ___

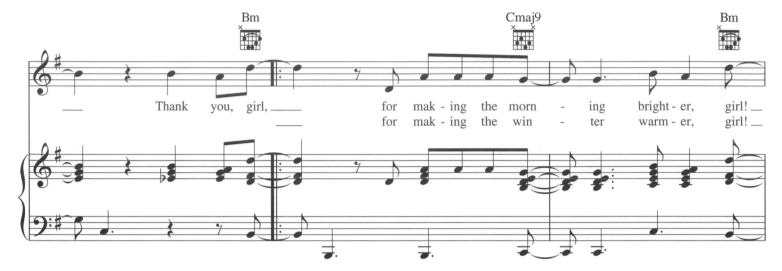

Thank you, girl, ___ for mak - ing the morn - ing bright - er, girl! ___
___ for mak - ing the win - ter warm - er, girl! ___

For mak - ing the night - time nic - er, girl! ___ For mak - ing a bet -
For mak - ing the mu - sic soft - er, girl! ___ For mak - ing a bet -

Repeat and Fade

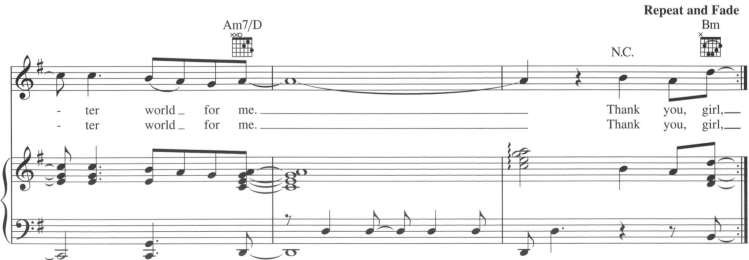

- ter world ___ for me. ___ Thank you, girl, ___
- ter world ___ for me. ___ Thank you, girl, ___

GOT TO BELIEVE IN MAGIC

Words by STEVE GEYER
Music by CHARLES FOX

Gently, but not too slowly

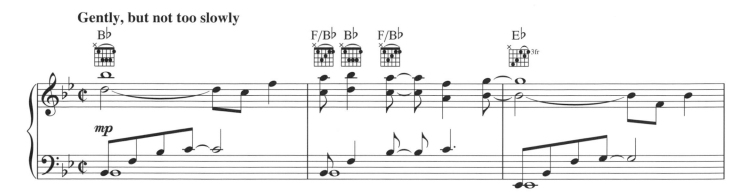

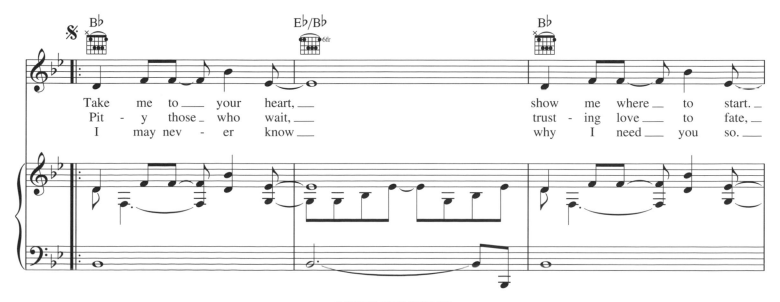

Take me to ___ your heart, ___ show me where ___ to start. ___
Pit - y those ___ who wait, ___ trust - ing love ___ to fate, ___
I may nev - er know ___ why I need ___ you so. ___

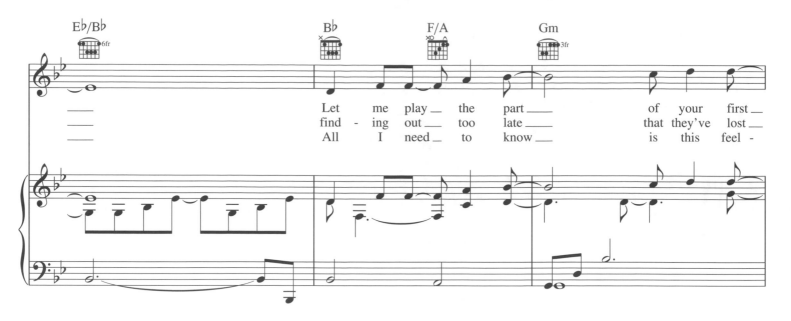

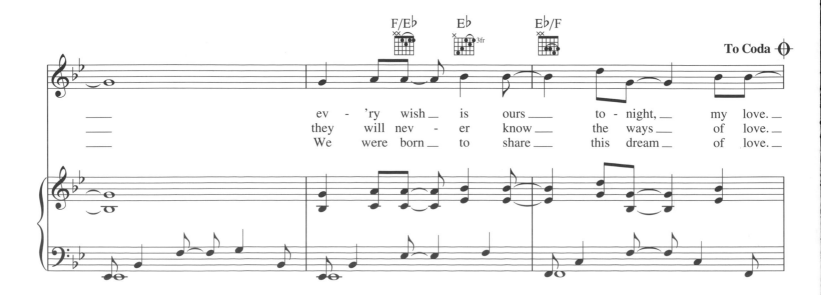

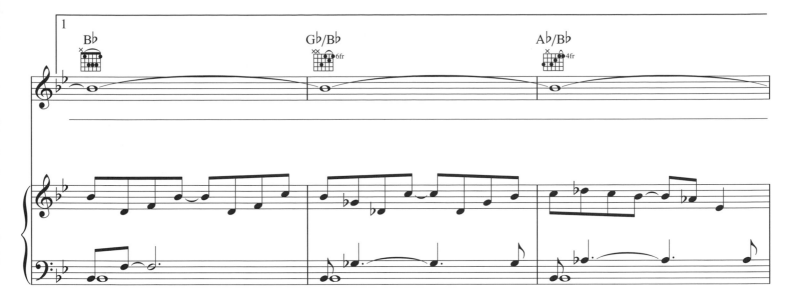

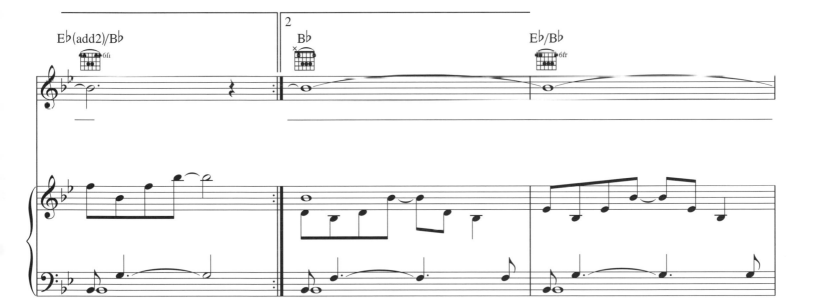

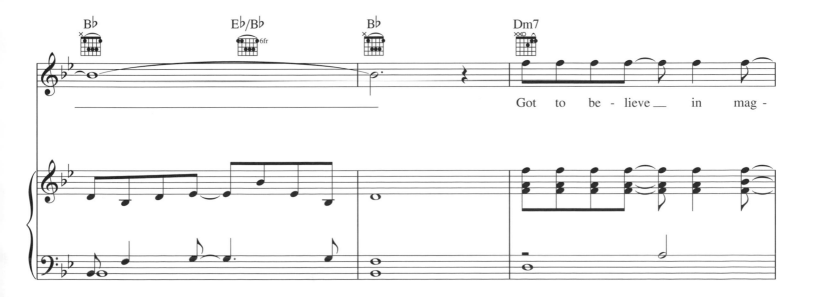

Got to be - lieve__ in mag -

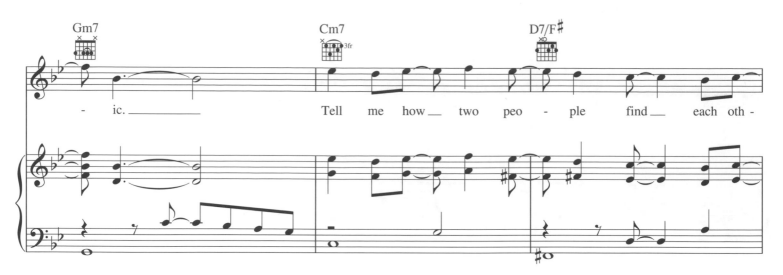

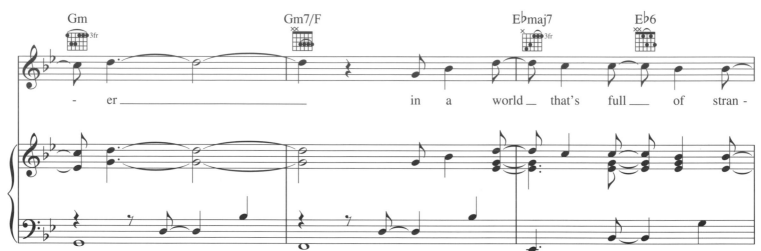

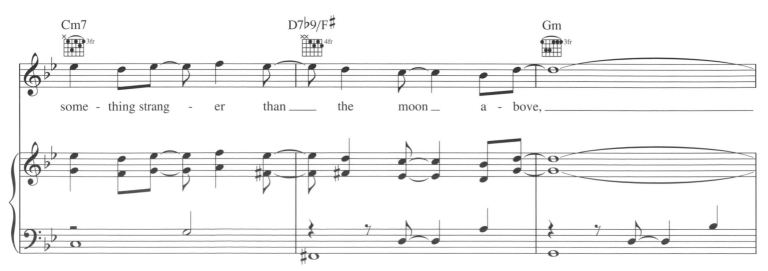

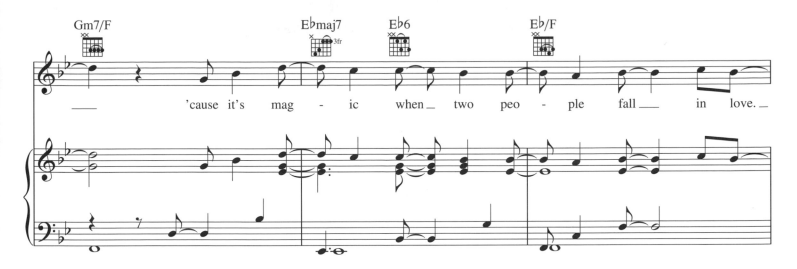

'cause it's mag - ic when two peo - ple fall in love.

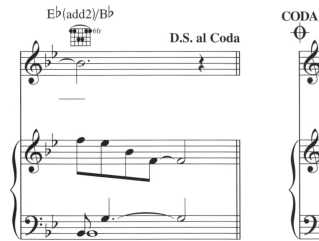

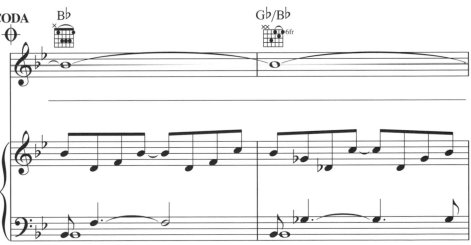

D.S. al Coda

CODA

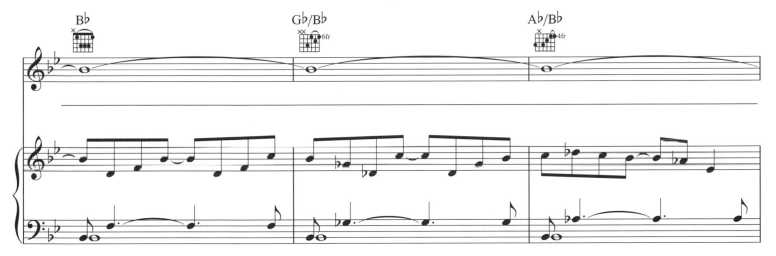

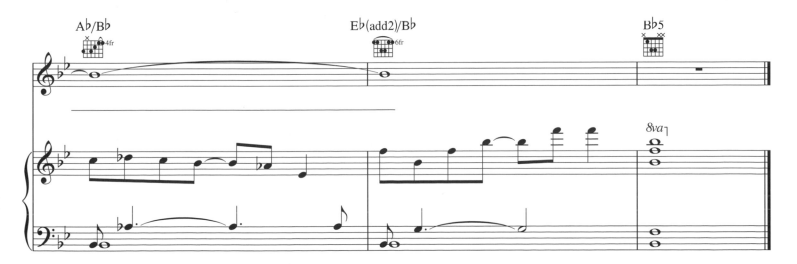

HAPPY DAYS

Theme from the Paramount Television Series HAPPY DAYS

Words by NORMAN GIMBEL
Music by CHARLES FOX

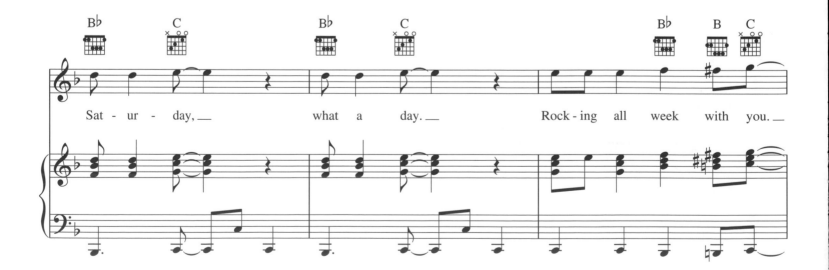

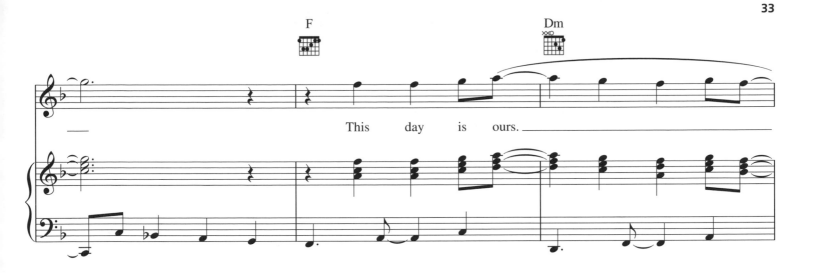

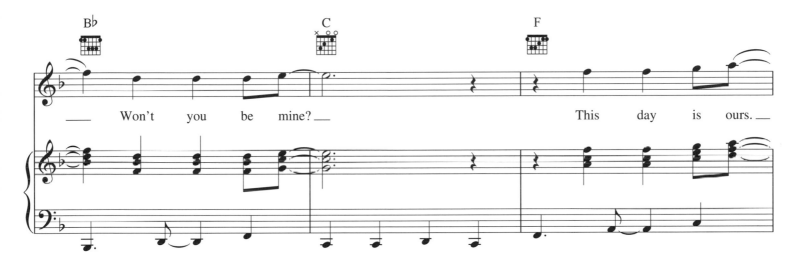

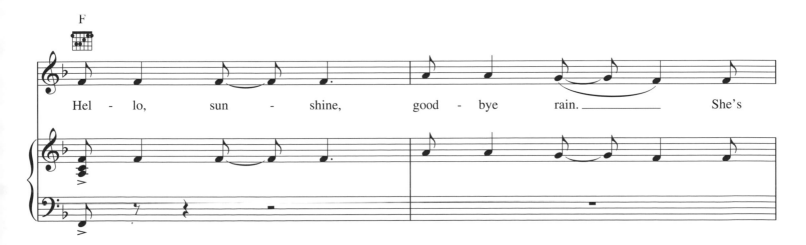

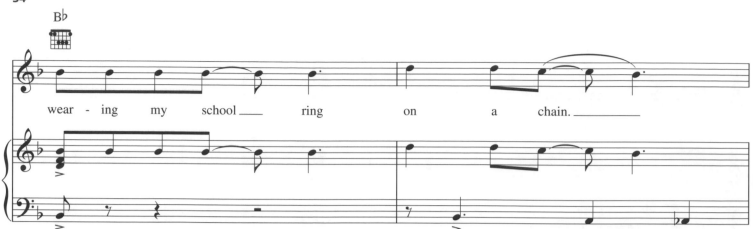

wear - ing my school ___ ring on a chain. _____

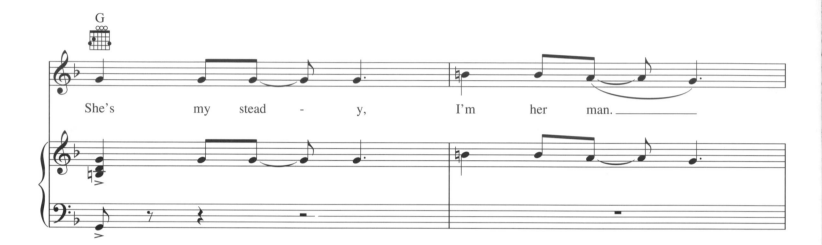

She's my stead - y, I'm her man. _____

I'm gon - na love her all ___ I can. ___ This day is ours. ___

_____ Won't you be mine? ___

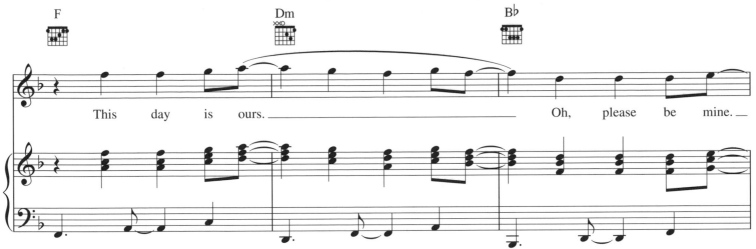

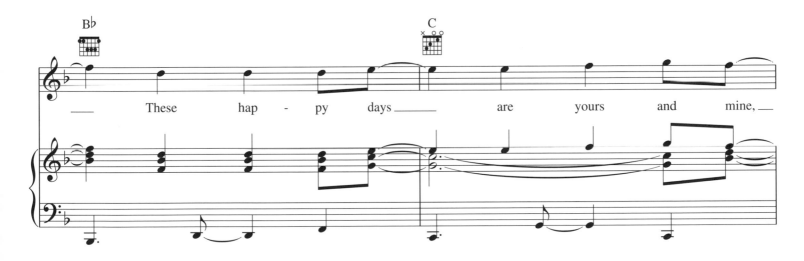

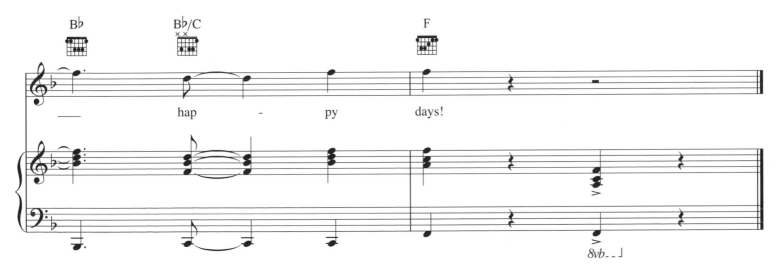

HOW DO I KNOW?

Words by DAVID ZIPPEL
Music by CHARLES FOX

I GO ALONG

Words by NORMAN GIMBEL
Music by CHARLES FOX

Moderately

The sun-light wakes___ me,_____
I think of you,___ friend,_____
I dream you're near___ me,_____

I go a-long___ with the sun;_____
And go a-long___ with my mind;_____
And go a-long___ with my dream;_____

Rise and shine___ bright as chrome,___ I dress___ and leave my home,___
You are the on - ly thing that's real,___ The on - ly one___ I feel,___
Helps me get in-to the night,___ To get___ in-to___ the light,___

To make my job.
You keep it sane.
Of one more day.

And when my job
And when my world
And when my day

be - gins to down me,
be - gins to down me,
be - gins to down me,

I think of you,
I think of you,
I think of you,

To Coda

1. I think of you.

2. I think of you. Too man-y days of my

I know if I'm_____ with you, then

I can get to that,_____ I've got to be where you__

are._____

D.S. al Coda

a tempo

Repeat and fade

Coda

I think_ of you._____

IT DIDN'T COME EASY

Words by NORMAN GIMBEL
Music by CHARLES FOX

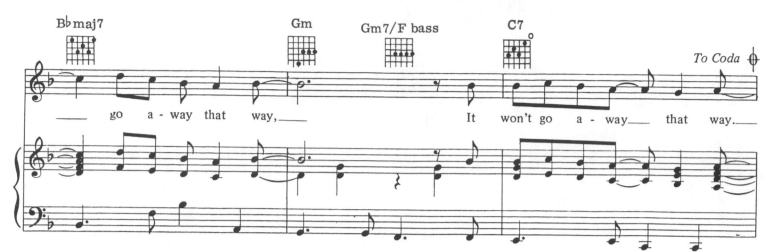

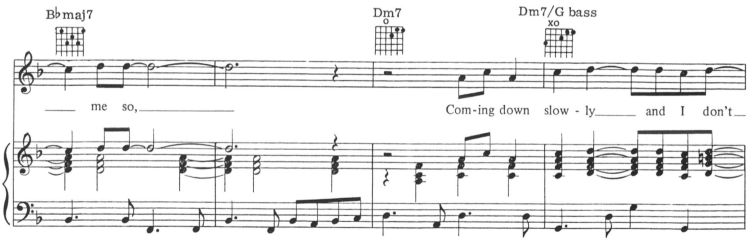

I GOT A NAME

from the 20th Century Fox Film LAST AMERICAN HERO

Words by NORMAN GIMBEL
Music by CHARLES FOX

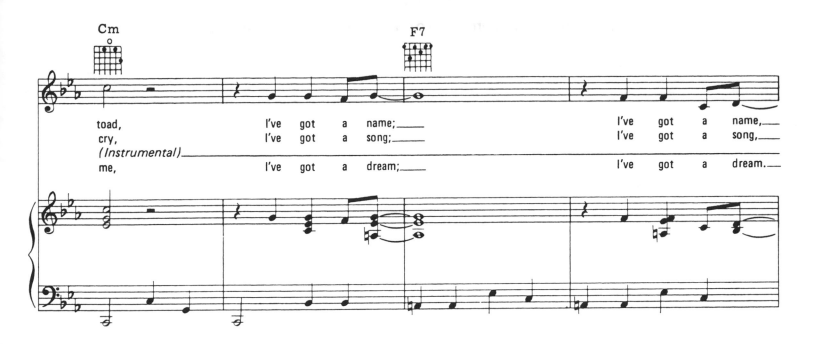

toad,   I've got a name;____   I've got a name,____
cry,   I've got a song;____   I've got a song,____
(Instrumental) ____
me,   I've got a dream;____   I've got a dream.____

and I car-ry it with____ me like my
and I car-ry it with____ me and I
(Instrumental) ____
Oh, I know I could share____ it if you'd

dad-dy did,____   but I'm liv-ing the dream____
sing it loud;____   if it gets me no where,____
(Instrumental) ____
want me to;____   if you're go-in' my____ way,____

52

3.

E♭

D. C. al 4th ending

And I'm gon-na go_____ there free._____

4.

Gm   A♭ 4 fr.   Gm

_____ Mov-in' me down the high - way,   roll-in' me down the high-

C7   A♭ 4 fr.   B♭

way,   mov-in' a-head so life_____ won't pass_____ me by._____

a tempo

E♭

KILLING ME SOFTLY WITH HIS SONG

Words by NORMAN GIMBEL
Music by CHARLES FOX

Moderately

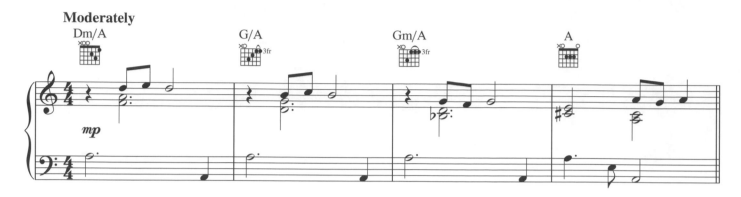

I heard __ he sang __ a good __ song, I heard he had
I felt __ all flushed __ with fe - ver, em - bar - rassed by __
He sang __ as if __ he knew __ me in all my dark __

__ a style, and so __ I came __ to see __ him to
__ the crowd. I felt __ he found __ my let - ters and
__ de - spair. And then __ he looked __ right through __ me as

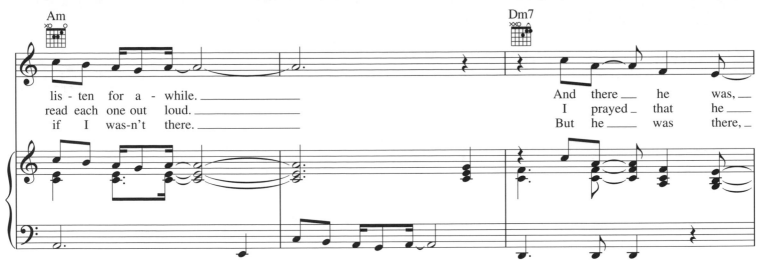

Am ... Dm7

lis - ten for a - while. _____
read each one out loud. _____
if I was-n't there. _____

And there ___ he was, ___
I prayed ___ that he ___
But he ___ was there, ___

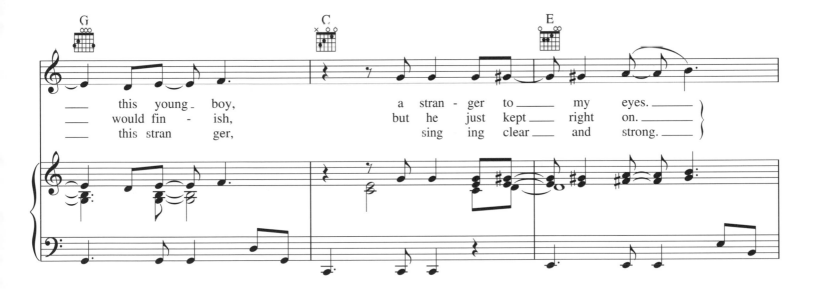

G ... C ... E

___ this young ___ boy,
___ would fin - ish,
___ this stran - ger,

a stran - ger to ___ my eyes. ___
but he just kept ___ right on. ___
sing - ing clear ___ and strong. ___

Am ... F ... G

Strum - ming my pain ___ with his fin - gers, _____   sing - ing my life ___ with his words. __

Kill - ing me soft - ly with his ___ song, kill - ing me soft -

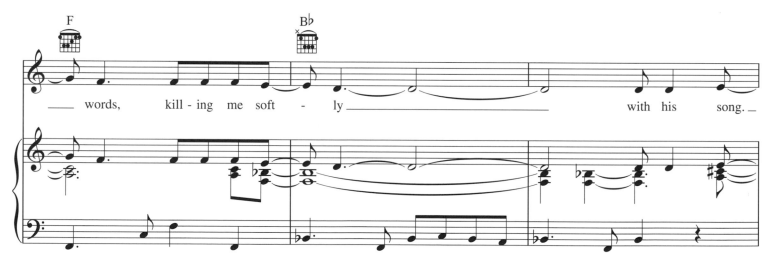

- ly ___ with his ___ song, tell - ing my whole ___ life ___ with his ___

___ words, kill - ing me soft - ly ___ with his song. ___

LOVE AMERICAN STYLE

Theme from the Paramount Television Series LOVE AMERICAN STYLE

Words and Music by ARNOLD MARGOLIN
and CHARLES FOX

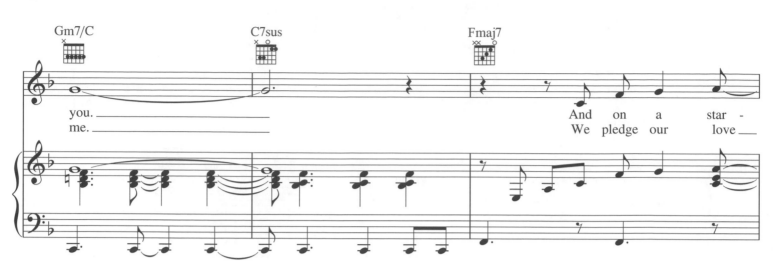

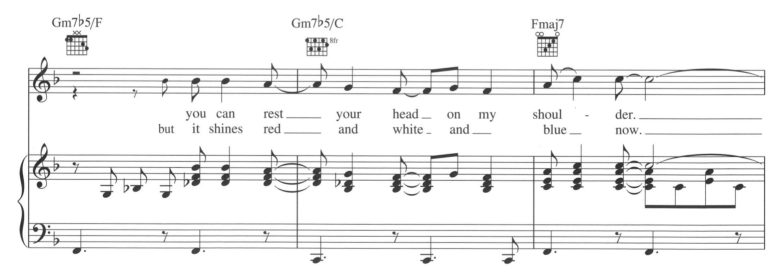

my love, I will de-fend
my love, all that I hope

your right to try.
for 'tis of thee.

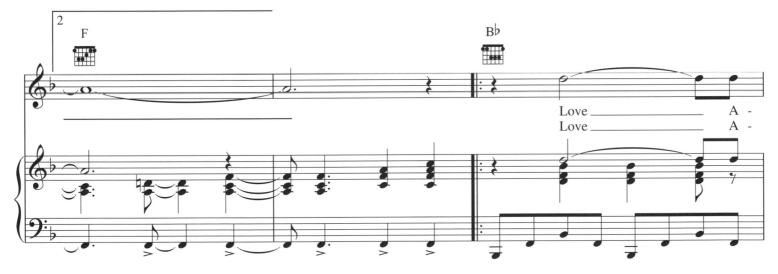

Love A-
Love A-

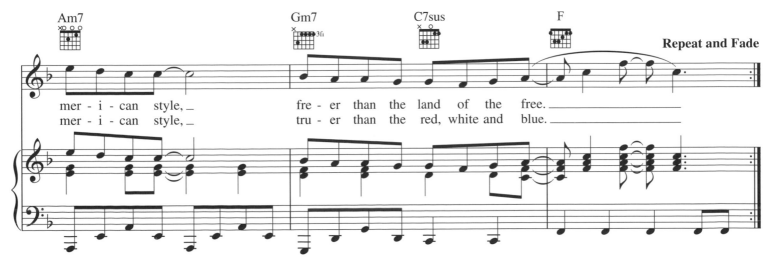

mer-i-can style, free-er than the land of the free.
mer-i-can style, tru-er than the red, white and blue.

LOVE BOAT THEME
from the Television Series

Words and Music by CHARLES FOX
and PAUL WILLIAMS

Moderate Disco

Love,

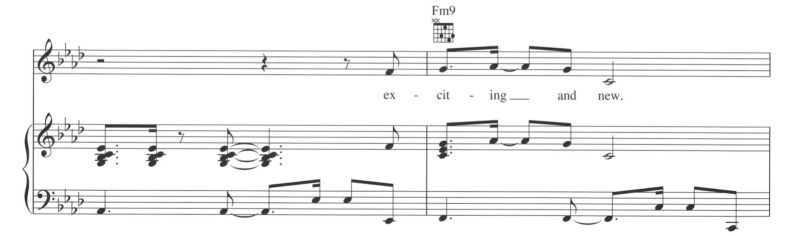

ex - cit - ing __ and new.

Come a - board,   we're ex -

pect - ing ___ you. ___ And ___

love, ___ life's

sweet - est re - ward. ___ Let it flow,

it ___ floats back to ___ you. ___

The Love Boat

soon will be mak-ing an-oth-er run. The

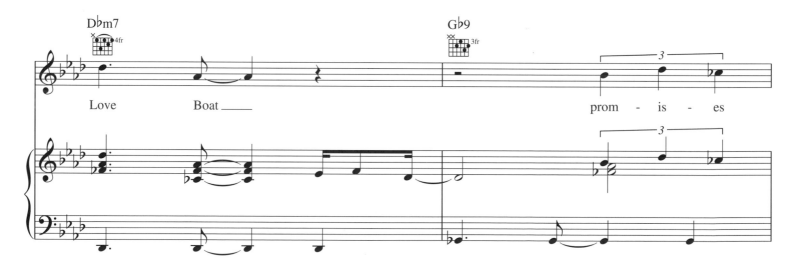

Love Boat prom - is - es

some - thing for ev - 'ry - one. Set a

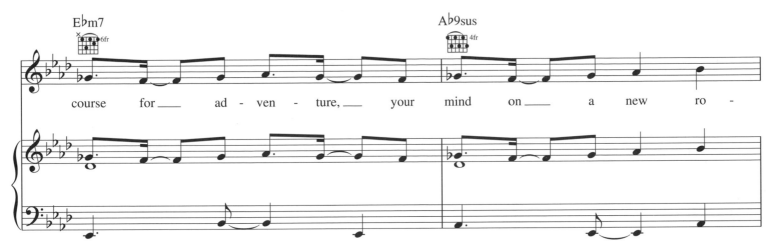

course for ___ ad - ven - ture, ___ your mind on ___ a new ro -

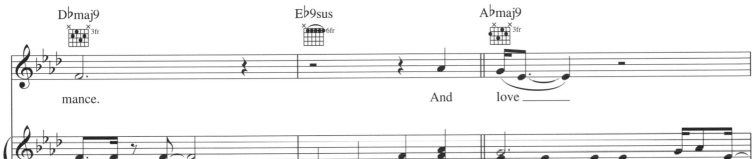

mance. And love ___

won't hurt ___ an - y - more. ___

It's ___ an o - pen ___ smile ___

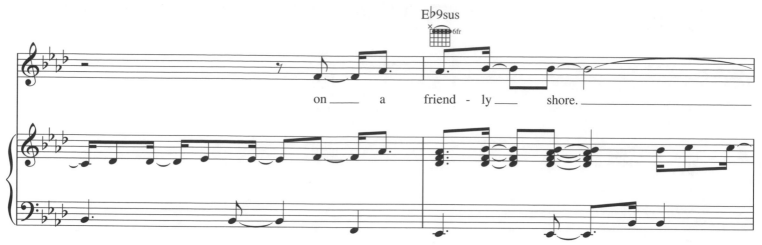

on _____ a friend - ly _____ shore. _____

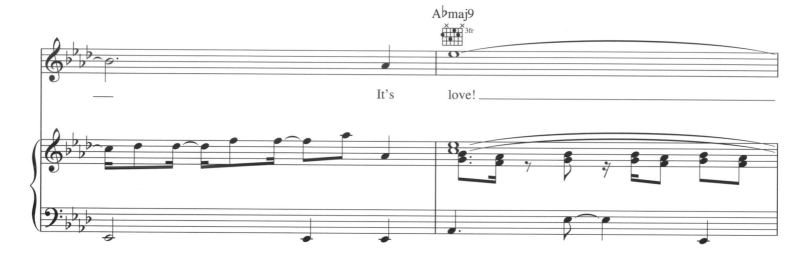

_____ It's love! _____

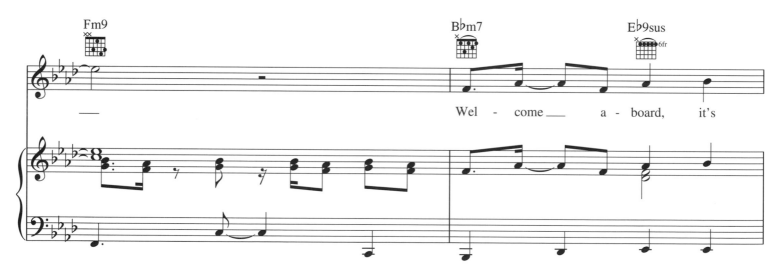

_____ Wel - come _____ a - board, it's

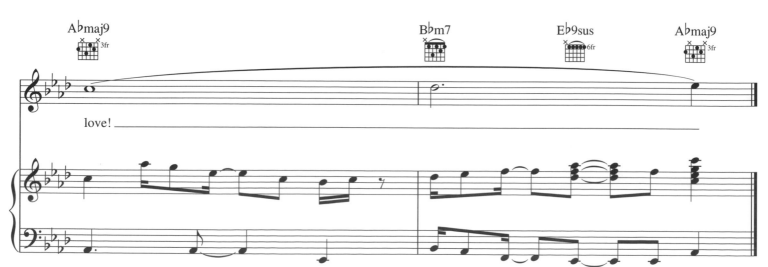

love! _____

MAKING OUR DREAMS COME TRUE

Theme from the Paramount Television Series LAVERNE AND SHIRLEY

Words by NORMAN GIMBEL
Music by CHARLES FOX

do - in' it our __ way. There is noth - ing we __ won't try; __

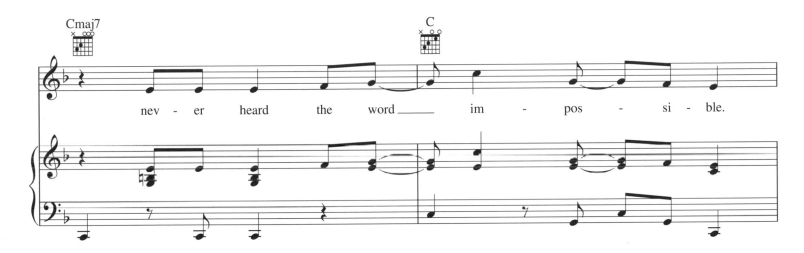

nev - er heard the word __ im - pos - si - ble.

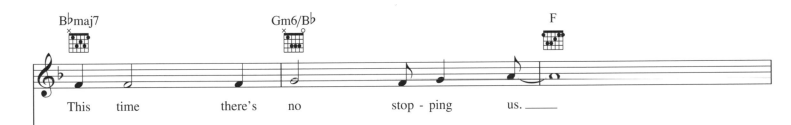

This time there's no stop - ping us. __

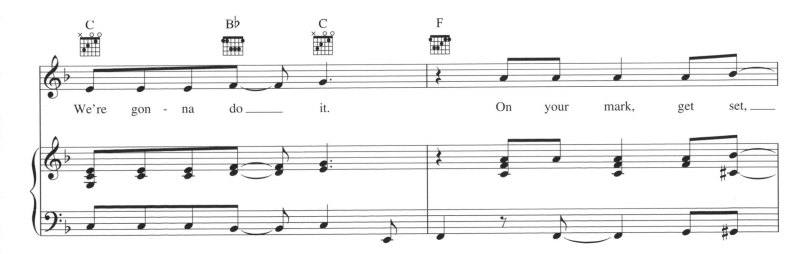

We're gon - na do __ it. On your mark, get set, __

and go now. Got a dream and we just know now,

we're gon - na make that dream come

true, and we'll do it our way, yes

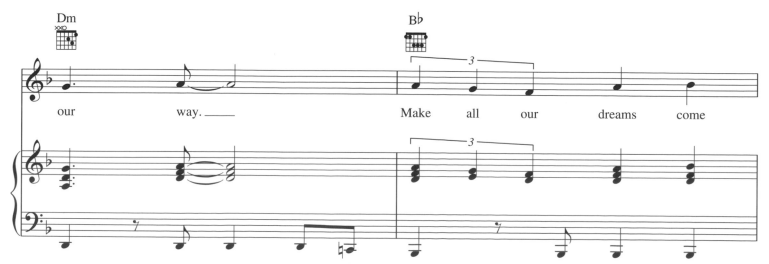

our way. Make all our dreams come

true, and do it our way, __ yes our way. __

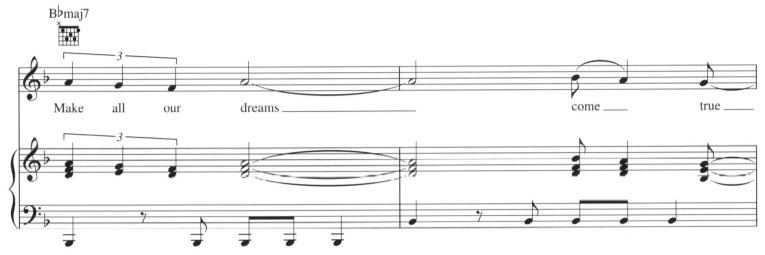

Make all our dreams _____ come __ true __

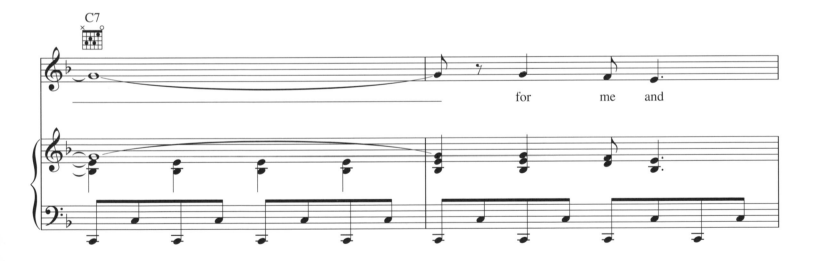

_____ for me and

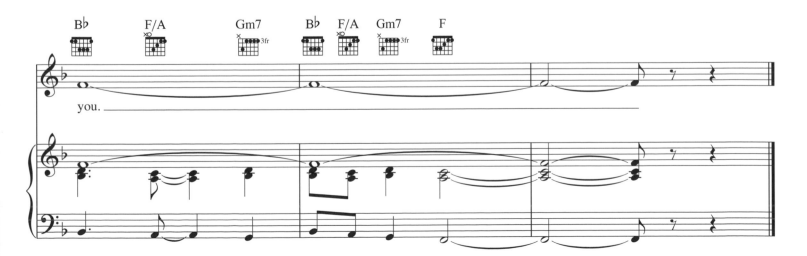

you. _____

MY FAIR SHARE

Words by PAUL WILLIAMS
Music by CHARLES FOX

READY TO TAKE A CHANCE AGAIN
(Love Theme)
from the Paramount Picture FOUL PLAY

Words by NORMAN GIMBEL
Music by CHARLES FOX

Moderately

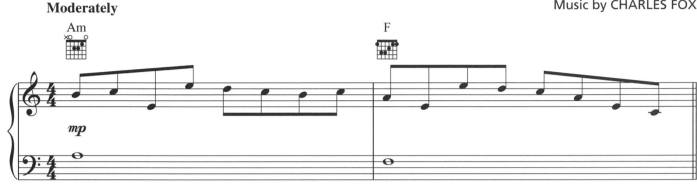

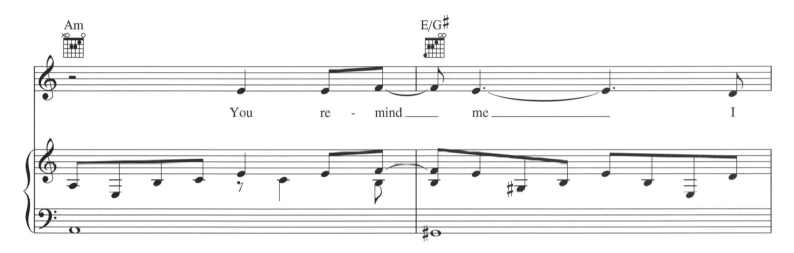

You re-mind _____ me _____ I

live in a shell, ___ safe from the past, ___

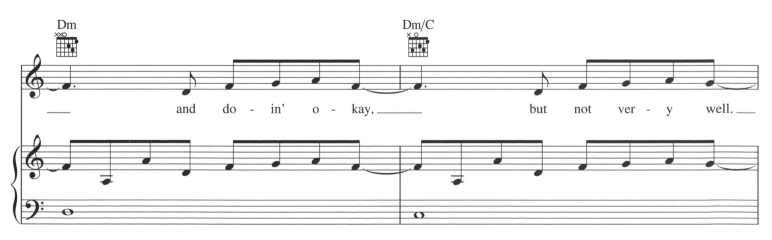

___ and do-in' o-kay, _____ but not ver-y well. ___

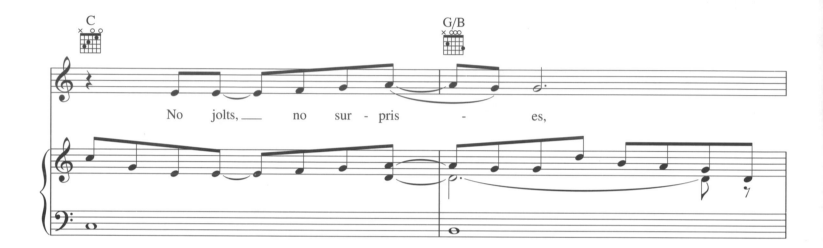

No jolts, ___ no sur - pris - es,

no cri - sis a - ris - es. My life ___ goes a - long ___

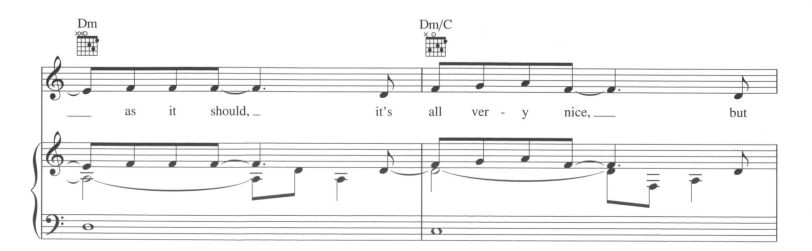

___ as it should, ___ it's all ver - y nice, ___ but

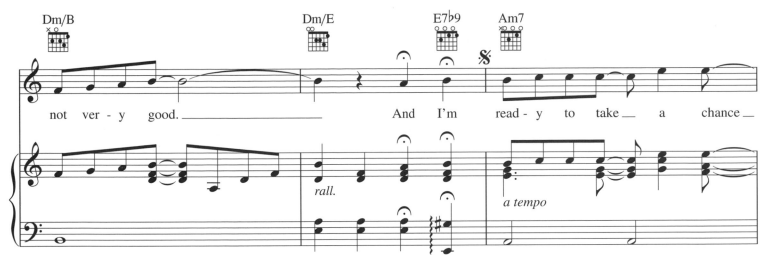

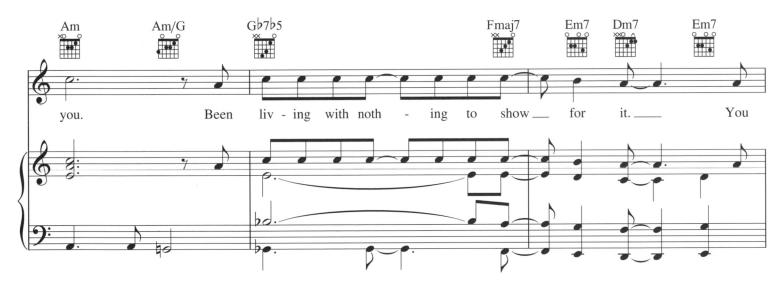

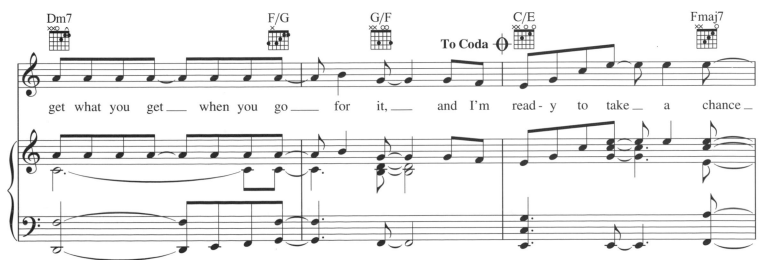

a - gain __ with __ you. _____

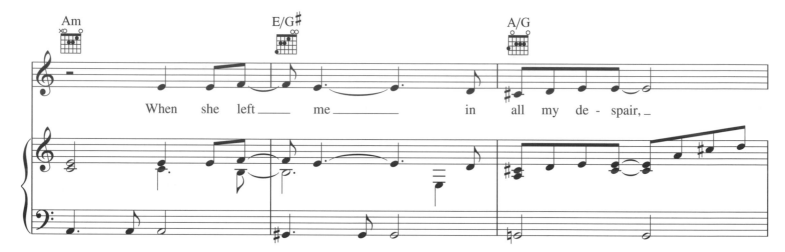

When she left ____ me ____ in all my de - spair, __

A7   Dm   Dm/C

I just held on. My hopes were all gone, _____ then

D.S. al Coda

I found you there. _____ And I'm

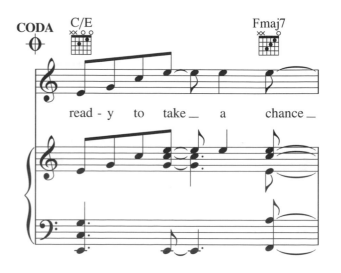

read - y to take __ a chance __

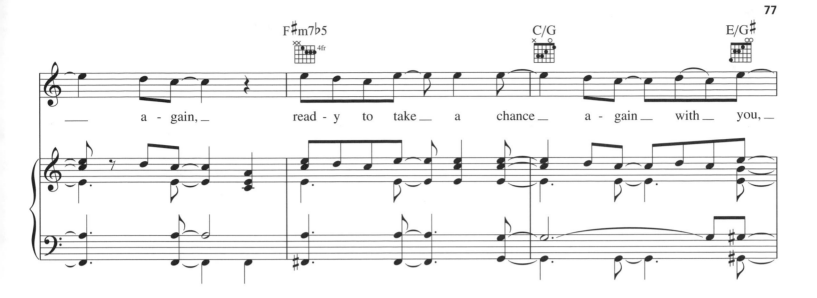

a - gain, __ read - y to take __ a chance __ a - gain __ with __ you, __

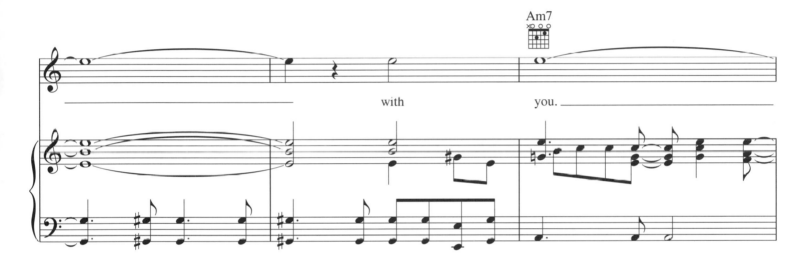

with you. __

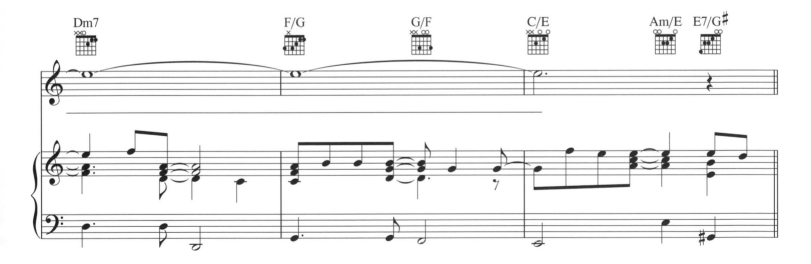

Repeat ad lib. and Fade

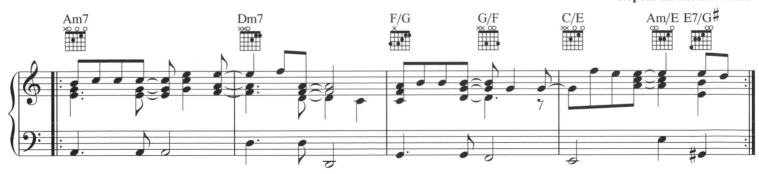

RICHARD'S WINDOW

Music by CHARLES FOX
Lyric by NORMAN GIMBEL

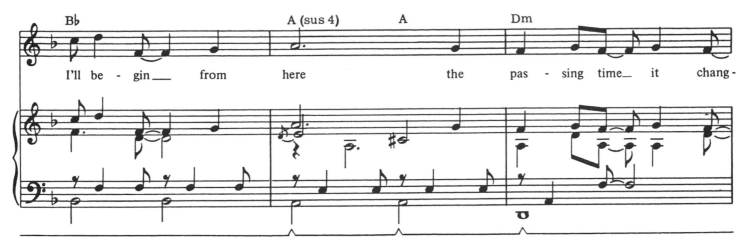

I'll be - gin___ from here   the pas - sing time___ it chang -

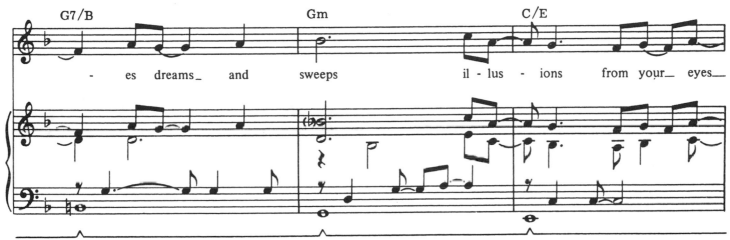

- es dreams___ and   sweeps   il - lus - ions   from your___ eyes___

He came to me___

___ to be a friend___   and I knew some - how___   he would - n't stay___

that he was some - one I___ could know___ a lit - tle while___

He brought a smile___ and he___ was free___

and he came to give___ it all___ to me___ the chance to see___

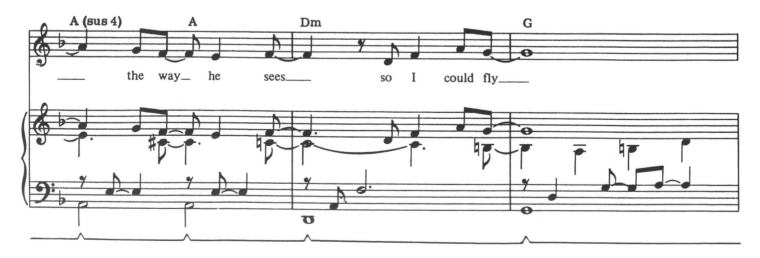

the way___ he sees___ so I could fly___

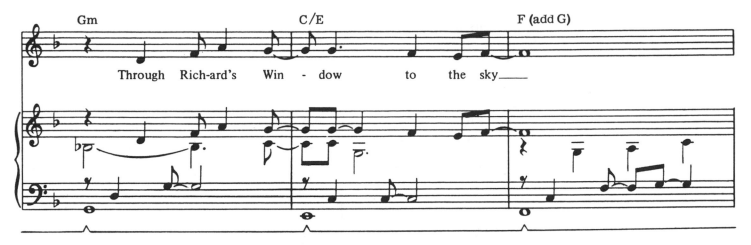

Through Rich-ard's Win - dow to the sky____

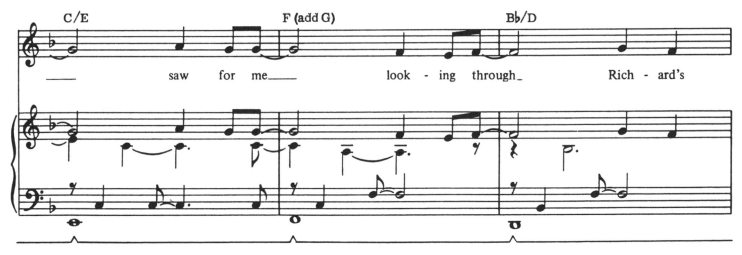

I try to see____ all that he____

____ saw for me____ look - ing through_ Rich - ard's

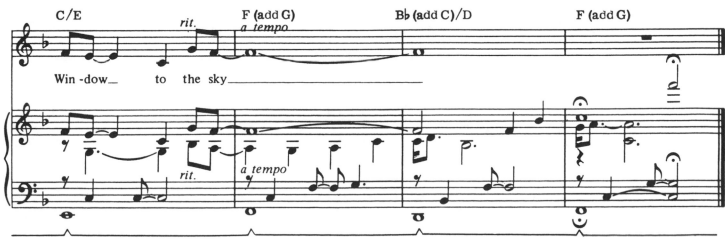

Win -dow_ to the sky____

SEASONS
Inspired by Pachelbel's Canon in D

Music by CHARLES FOX
and ED NEWMAN

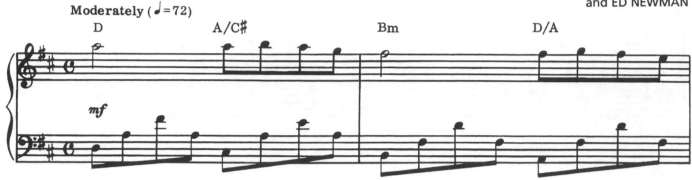

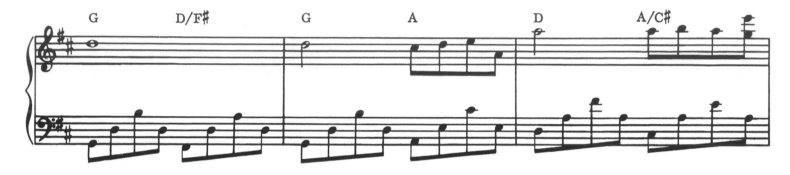

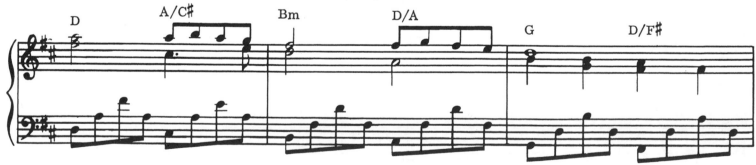

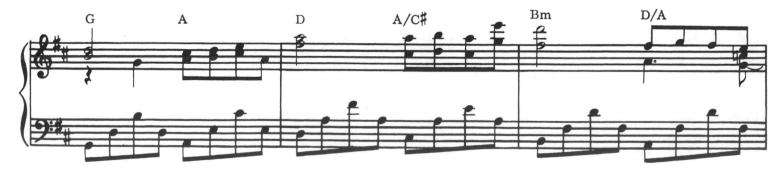

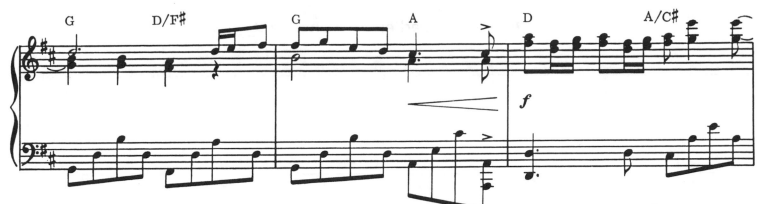

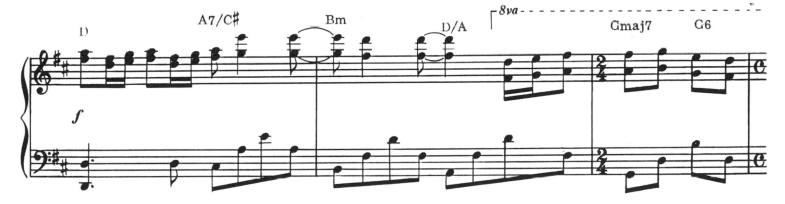

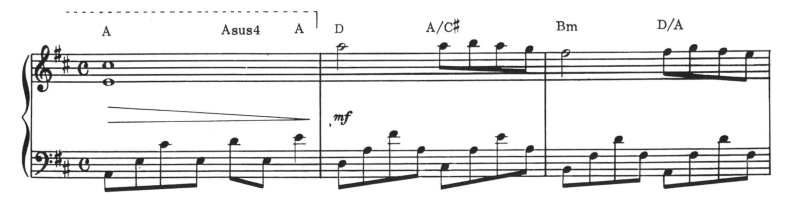

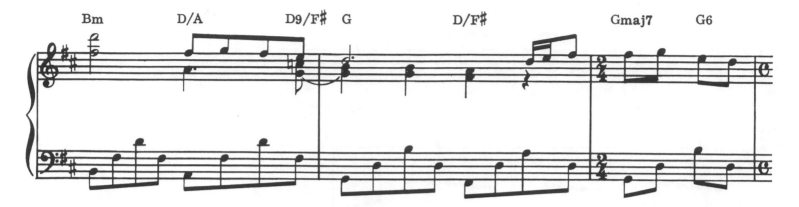

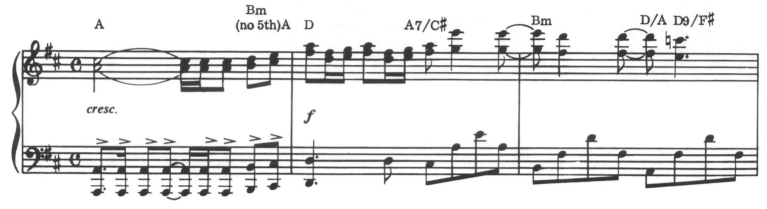

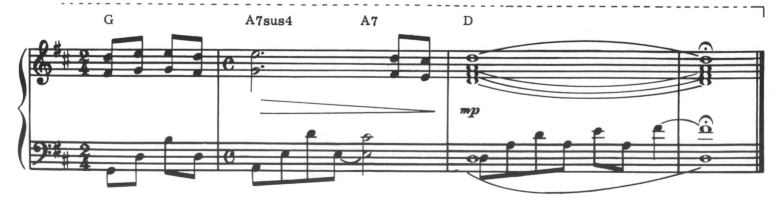

TOGETHER

Words by NORMAN GIMBEL
Music by CHARLES FOX

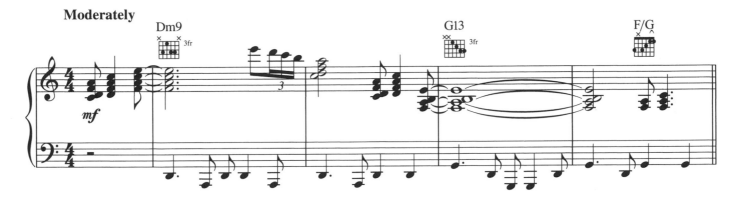

She/He clos-es her/his eyes ___ and she/he makes mu - sic. ___
I tell her/him my dreams _ and all my se - crets. ___

She/He clos-es her/his eyes ___ and I close mine.
I tell her/him my dreams _ and she/he tells hers. ___/his. ___

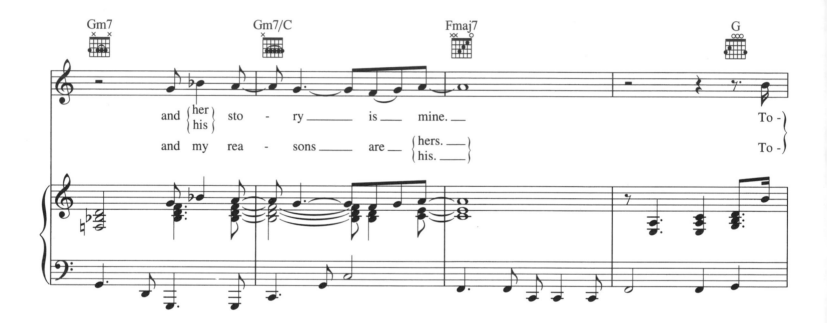

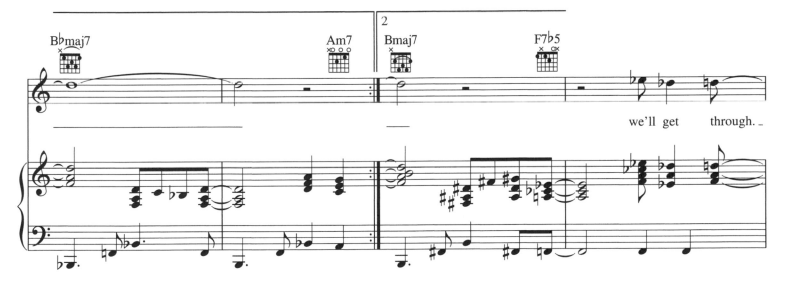

THERE'S A HARBOR

Words by NORMAN GIMBEL
Music by CHARLES FOX

Moderately

Cmaj7 (Ebmaj7)
Fmaj7 (Abmaj7)
C/G bass (Eb/Bb bass)

There's a har-bor gon-na sail___ to ___
There's a har-bor gon-na come___ to ___

E7 sus4 (G7 sus4) E7 (G7) Am (Cm) Am/G bass (Cm/Bb bass)

some-day___
some-day___

On the tail of an East___ wind some-day.___
Gon-na an-chor my boat___ down some-day.___

F (Ab) F/G bass (Ab/Bb bass) Em7 (Gm7)

And I'll___ be___ home,___
And I'll just walk a-shore,___

* Guitarists, capo up 3 frets

WE COULD HAVE IT ALL

from the Universal Film THE LAST MARRIED COUPLE IN AMERICA

Words by NORMAN GIMBEL
Music by CHARLES FOX

WONDER WOMAN

from the Warner Bros. TV Series WONDER WOMAN

Words by NORMAN GIMBEL
Music by CHARLES FOX

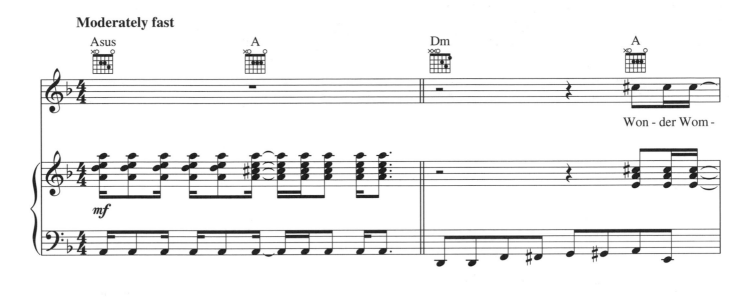

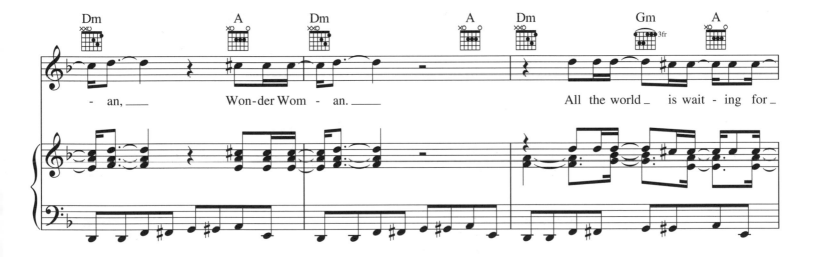

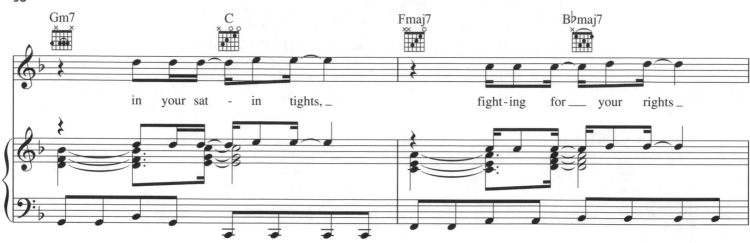

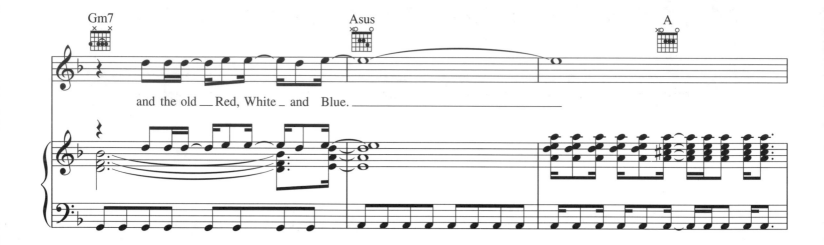

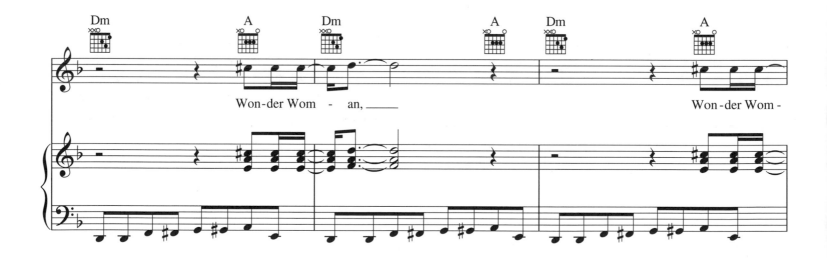

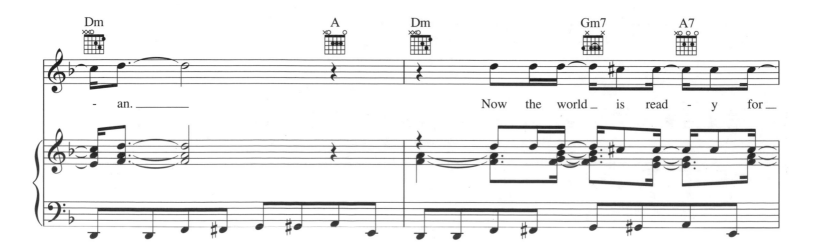

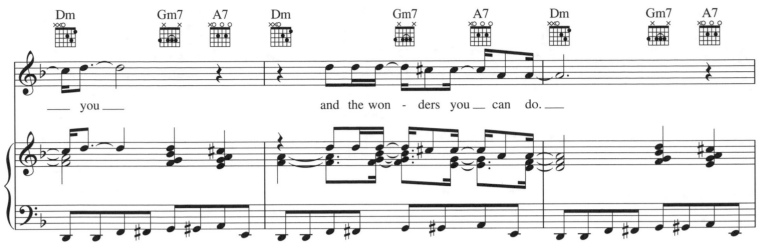

Get us out___ from un - der, Won - der Wom-

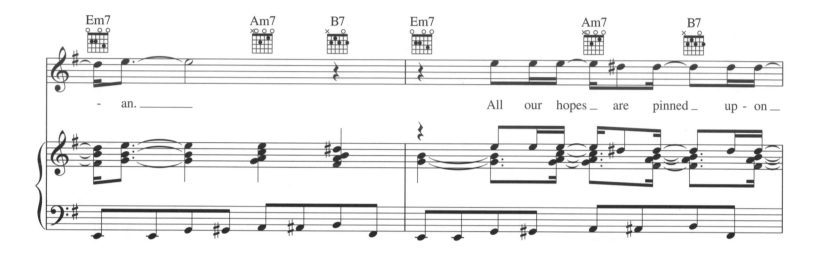

- an. ___ All our hopes___ are pinned___ up - on___

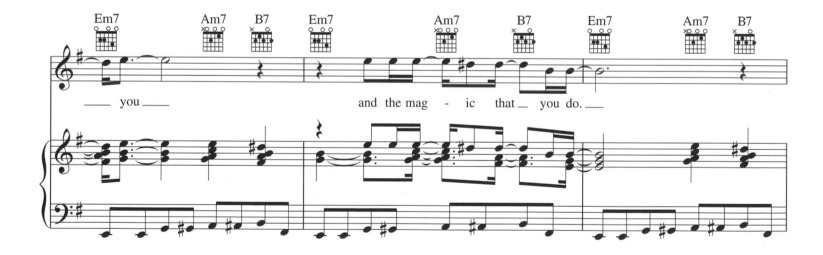

___ you ___ and the mag - ic that___ you do. ___

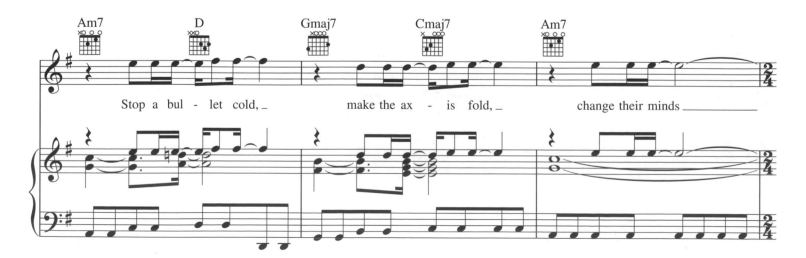

Stop a bul - let cold, ___ make the ax - is fold, ___ change their minds ___

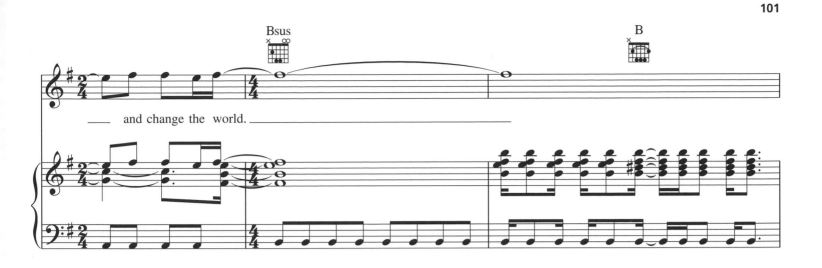

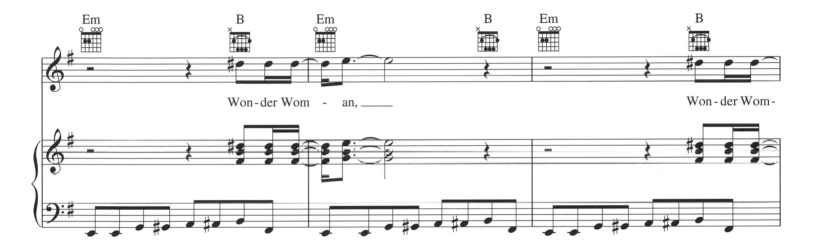

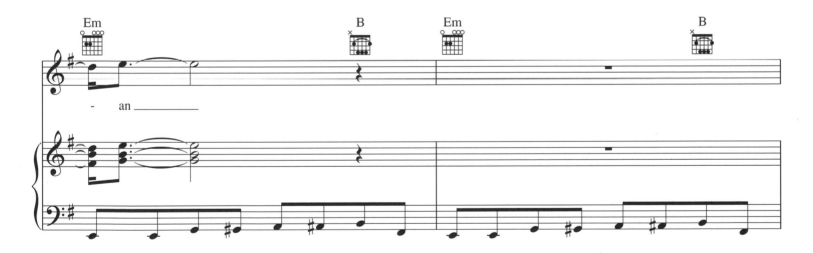